WHALE SHARKS

THE SHARK DISCOVERY LIBRARY

Sarah Palmer

Illustrated by Ernest Nicol and Libby Turner

Rourke Enterprises, Inc.
Vero Beach, Florida 32964

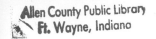
Library of Congress Cataloging-in-Publication Data

Palmer, Sarah, 1955-
    Whale Sharks/Sarah Palmer; illustrated by Ernest Nicol
and Libby Turner

        p. cm. — (Sharks discovery library)
    Includes index.
    Summary: An introduction to the whale shark, the
biggest fish in the world — but harmless to people.
    ISBN 0-86592-463-5
    1. Whale Shark—Juvenile literature.   [1. Whale Shark.
2. Sharks] I. Nicol, Ernest, ill. II. Title.
III. Series: Palmer,Sarah,1955-
Sharks discovery library.
QL638.95.R4P35   1989   88-4609
597'.31 - dc19   CIP
                                 AC

TABLE OF CONTENTS

Whale Sharks 5

How They Look 6

Where They Live 9

What They Eat 11

Their Jaws and Teeth 14

Baby Whale Sharks 16

Whale Sharks and Man 19

Their Skin 20

Fact File 22

Glossary 23

Index 24

WHALE SHARKS

Whale sharks are the biggest fish in the world. They have often been mistaken for whales because of their enormous size. Whale sharks cruise slowly through the water. They never seem to hurry. Whale sharks have often been seen resting lazily on the surface of the ocean. Today whale sharks are quite rare.

A whale shark swims lazily at the surface

HOW THEY LOOK

Whale sharks have dark green-gray backs with pale yellow spots. Their undersides are white. Whale sharks have broad, flat heads and a very wide mouth. Their huge bodies are rounded, with ridges running from the head to the tail along the back. An average male whale shark is about 27 feet long. The largest whale shark ever known measured over 41 feet long.

Whale sharks have very wide mouths

WHERE THEY LIVE

Whale sharks like to live in warm waters. They are found in **tropical oceans**, both far out to sea and near to shore. Whale sharks have been seen along the east coast of the United States and off California. Many whale sharks are found in the Gulf of Mexico at certain times of the year. They are most common in the Indian Ocean.

Whale sharks live in warm waters

WHAT THEY EAT

Whale sharks spend their days feeding on tiny plants called **plankton** and small shrimp-like creatures known as **krill**. They also eat some kinds of fish and squid. The whale sharks open their mouths and swallow whatever goes in. Sometimes they eat garbage by mistake. Buckets, boots, oars, and other such objects have all been found in the stomachs of whale sharks!

Whale sharks eat schools of fish

Whale sharks sometimes ea[t]
garbage

Whale sharks are not dangerous

THEIR JAWS AND TEETH

Whale sharks have more than 300 bands of tiny teeth. The teeth are much too small for the sharks to eat very big fish, and the whale sharks' mouths do not open wide enough. The sharks feed on plankton and krill, which they take into their mouths with the sea water. The water is pushed out through the whale sharks' **gill slits**, leaving the food in their mouths to be swallowed.

Whale sharks have many sma̵
teeth

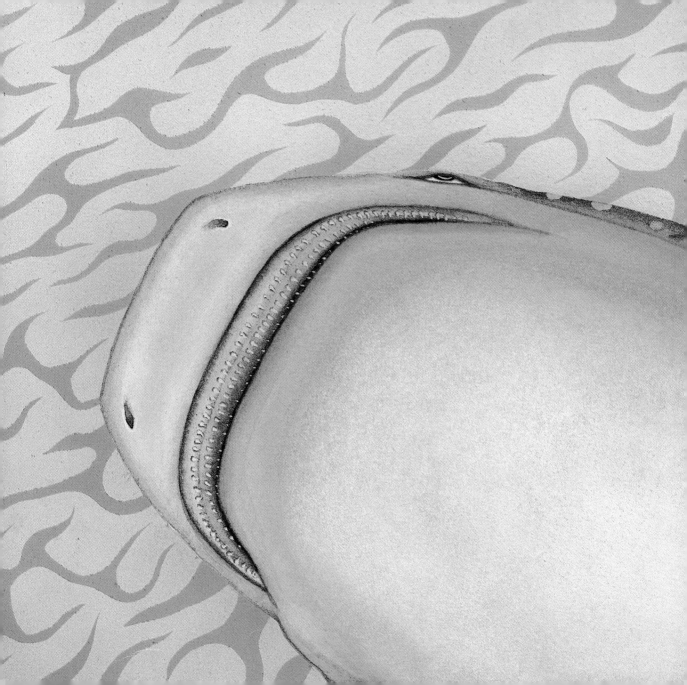

BABY WHALE SHARKS

Scientists are still studying all kinds of sharks to learn more about how the babies are born. We know that the mother whale shark produces oblong-shaped eggs. The baby whale sharks grow inside the eggs. After the eggs are laid, the baby sharks hatch from them. People have found some whale sharks' eggs that were nearly 20 inches long.

Baby whale sharks hatch from eggs

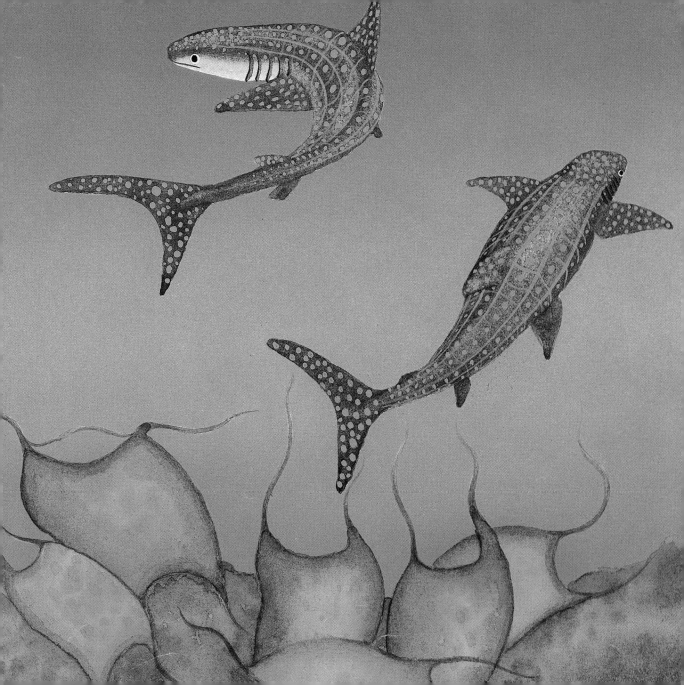

WHALE SHARKS AND MAN

In spite of their size, the huge whale sharks are quite harmless. Their sharp little teeth could hurt you if you were not careful, but whale sharks are not at all **aggressive**. They seem to like people and play happily with them in the water. Whale sharks let divers hold onto their fins and take a ride through the water. They are very gentle when they play.

*Whale sharks sometimes give
divers rides on their fins*

THEIR SKIN

Sharks' skin is covered with scales, which are sometimes called **denticles**. Each kind of shark has differently shaped scales. Scientists can tell what kind of shark they are looking at by the scaly skin. The scales, or denticles, grow backward along the body, much like fur on an animal. If you stroke a shark's body from front to back, it feels smooth. But if you rub it the other way, it is very rough and hurts your hand.

Sharks' skin is made of scales called denticles

FACT FILE

Common Name: Whale Shark

Scientific Name: Rhiniodon typus

Color: Greenish gray with yellow spots

Average Size: Male   – 29 feet, 6 inches
Female – 26 feet, 3 inches

Where They Live: Warm waters, inshore and oceans

Danger Level: No danger

Glossary

aggressive (ag GRES sive) — likely to attack

denticles (DEN ti cles) — scales on a shark's back

gill slits (GILL SLITS) — openings where water taken in
through the mouth passes back into the sea

krill (KRILL) — tiny shrimp-like creatures on which sharks feed

plankton (PLANK ton) — tiny plants on which sharks feed

tropical oceans (TRO pi cal OC eans) — warm seas close to
the equator

INDEX

babies	16
color	22
denticles	20
feeding	11
size	5, 19, 22
skin	20
teeth	14, 19